Parent's Introduction

We Both Read is the first series of books designed to invite parents and children to share the reading of a story by taking turns reading aloud. This "shared reading" innovation, which was developed in conjunction with early reading specialists, invites parents to read the more sophisticated text on the left-hand pages, while children are encouraged to read the right-hand pages, which have been written at one of three early reading levels.

Reading aloud is one of the most important activities parents can share with their child to assist their reading development. However, *We Both Read* goes beyond reading *to* a child and allows parents to share reading *with* a child. *We Both Read* is so powerful and effective because it combines two key elements in learning: "showing" (the parent reads) and "doing" (the child reads). The result is not only faster reading development for the child, but a much more enjoyable and enriching experience for both!

Most of the words used in the child's text should be familiar to them. Others can easily be sounded out. An occasional difficult word will be first introduced in the parent's text, distinguished with **bold lettering**. Pointing out these words, as you read them, will help familiarize them to your child. You may also find it helpful to read the entire book aloud yourself the first time, then invite your child to participate on the second reading. Also note that the parent's text is preceded by a "talking parent" icon: ⮾ ; and the child's text is preceded by a "talking child" icon: ⮿ .

We Both Read books is a fun, easy way to encourage and help your child to read — and a wonderful way to start your child off on a lifetime of reading enjoyment!

We Both Read: About The Rain Forest

Use of photographs provided by James L. Castner, Louisa Preston, Photo Disc,
Corbis Images, Animals/Animals; Zig Leszczynski, Gerard Lacz, Michael Dick,
Dani/Jeske, Austin Stevens, Joe McDonald, Patti Murray, Ken Cole, Fogden,
M OSF, Doug Wechsler, Raymond A. Mendez, Betty K. Bruce, David Haring,
J. & P. Wegner. Earth Sciences: Michael Fogden

We Both Read™ is a trademark of Treasure Bay, Inc.

Published by Treasure Bay, Inc.
17 Parkgrove Drive
South San Francisco, CA 94080 USA

PRINTED IN SINGAPORE

Library of Congress Catalog Number: 99 076875

Hardcover ISBN 1-891327-23-2
Paperback ISBN 1-891327-24-0

FIRST EDITION

We Both Read™ Books
Patent No. 5,957,693

About The Rain Forest

By Heather Johanasen
and Sindy McKay

TREASURE BAY

We are about to go deep into a most unusual forest full of adventure, a forest filled with mysteries to be solved and treasures to be saved. This forest is called the **tropical rain forest**.

Located in the warm areas around the world's equator, the tropical rain forests of the world are filled with animals and plants found nowhere else on earth.

It rains a lot in a **tropical rain forest**.

The air is always wet and warm.

It feels like summer all year long.

A rain forest is made up of several layers. The first layer is called the **forest floor**. It's filled with leaves, ferns and small bushes.

The second layer is called the **understory**. Small trees and strong vines create the body of the rain forest, making nice homes for many small animals.

The final layer, made up of the tallest trees in the forest, is the **canopy**. These tall trees are home for many exotic birds and monkeys.

 The **canopy** of the forest gets a lot of sun.

Some sun passes through the canopy to reach the **understory**.

The **forest floor** gets only a little bit of sun.

Some trees in the rain forest **grow** very tall trying to reach up to the sun, some as high as 200 feet. That's as tall as a 20-story building!

To help support this great height, wings of hardwood called buttress roots **grow** out from the base of the tree above the forest floor. These roots alone can **grow** twice as tall as a person.

Monkey Ladder Vine

 This vine **grows** in the understory of the rain forest.

People call it a monkey ladder.

It looks like it has steps a monkey could use.

The **marmoset** is a breed of monkey commonly found in the rain forest. These playful animals have earned the nickname "gremlin" for their mischievous behavior, and are often kept as pets by the native people.

This pygmy **marmoset** is the smallest monkey in the world.

These little monkeys live in families.

The father helps the mother take care of the babies.

Often confused for monkeys, **lemurs** are adorable little animals with long bushy tails and big, wide eyes.

The aye-aye is a rare kind of **lemur** that lives in the rain forest on the island of Madagascar, off the coast of Africa. It hunts at night, using its unusually long hook fingers to help him find bugs underneath tree bark.

Some **lemurs** have black rings on their tails.

They are called "ring tail lemurs".

They live and play in groups.

They like to eat fruit.

The **orangutan** is a great ape that lives in the rain forests of Asia.

The largest tree-dwelling animal on earth, **orangutans** have very long and powerful arms. These arms help them to move easily through the **branches** of the rain forest canopy where they spend most of their time.

The name **orangutan** means "people of the forest".

Mother Orangutan and Baby

An **orangutan** baby rides on its mother's back.

It uses its feet like hands.

It can use its feet to grab **branches** and pick fruit.

Rain forests are full of beautifully colored snakes. Some are venomous, meaning they kill their prey by injecting poison. **Boa** snakes are constrictors, meaning they suffocate their prey by squeezing them with their powerful bodies.

One type of boa is the **emerald tree boa**, which can be up to 10 feet long!

The **emerald tree boa** is bright green.

Its green body helps it to hide in the trees all day.

It comes out at night to hunt.

It hunts rats and birds.

Can you imagine a guinea pig the size of a big dog? Then you can imagine a **capybara**! The **capybara** is the largest rodent in the world—some weighing over 100 lbs!

The **capybara** has no tail, fur that's long and coarse, and very strong claws. It uses its claws to pull up the water plants it finds near rivers and **ponds**.

Capybara Mother and Baby

Capybaras are very good swimmers.

They live near rivers and **ponds**.

They go under the water when they need to hide.

Their feet are webbed, just like a duck!

Giant water **lily** pads grow in rain forest lakes. Many grow big enough for a small child to sit on, some up to 6 feet wide.

The Queen Victoria water **lily** grows in dark shallow water. Birds can use the **lily** pads to rest on and to stay protected from hungry water creatures.

Amazon Water Lily

 The water **lily** flower changes color.

It starts out being white.

It turns purple when the sun comes up!

Panther Chameleon

For some rain forest creatures, playing hide and seek is no problem at all! Chameleons and **katydids** use shape and color to hide from their enemies and to sneak up on their prey.

Chameleons can change their color to blend in with their surroundings. This natural disguise is called camouflage.

There are many different kinds of **katydids**.

This one looks like a leaf.

Looking like a leaf, helps it to hide.

Can you find the katydid in this picture?

Rain forest birds such as the macaw and the **toucan** are brilliantly colored. These bright colors help them attract other birds.

Macaws are very large parrots that live in South American rain forests. Males have especially bright feathers that catch the attention of female macaws.

 **Toucans** have big, colorful bills.

They like to eat fruit.

They also like to play games.

They play by tossing fruit back and forth to each other!

Cats come in many sizes in the rain forest. One of the smallest is the **margay**. One of the largest is the jaguar, which can weigh up to 300 pounds!

Jaguars are excellent swimmers—and they like to fish! The jaguar can dangle his tail in the water and when a fish comes to investigate, the jaguar can snatch it up in its powerful jaws.

Margay

 **Margays** love to climb in trees.

They can climb down trees head first.

At night margays hunt for food.

They eat small birds and rats.

 Did you know that rubber balls and chocolate bars both come from trees in the rain forest?

Chocolate comes from the **cocoa** trees. Rubber, called latex, comes from the sap of the rubber tree.

When the bark of the rubber tree is cut, latex slowly drips down into a cup. Cutting the bark doesn't hurt the rubber tree at all.

Cocoa Fruit Pod

The seeds of the **cocoa** fruit are used to make **chocolate**.

Rain forest animals love to eat this sweet fruit!

Some of the most colorful frogs in the world live in the South American rain forest. But some of these cute little creatures can also be very **dangerous**.

This strawberry poison dart frog is a very poisonous creature. It doesn't bite like a snake does. The poison comes out of pores on its skin, so just touching this frog can be bad news!

This red-eyed tree frog is not **dangerous** at all.

Like all frogs, it started life in the water as a tadpole.

When it became a frog, it moved up into the trees of the rain forest.

Short-nosed Fruit Bats

When most of us think of bats, we think of scary creatures that live in caves and only come out on Halloween night. But the **flying fox** is a breed of fruit bat that sleeps out in the sun, hanging upside-down from trees high above the rain forest floor—sometimes in "camps" made up of as many as a million bats!

Flying Fox

 Most bats do not see very well.

Many bats eat bugs.

But **flying foxes** can see very well,
and they eat fruit and flowers.

Sometimes slimy and always slow is a good way to describe the three-toed **sloth**. It moves so slowly that if it were to race a snail the snail just might win!

Algae grows in the **sloth's** fur, creating a green tint. This subtle color helps the sloth to blend in with the rain forest canopy where it lives.

Three-toed Sloth

 The **sloth** loves to hang upside down in trees.

It eats leaves and flowers.

Sometimes it falls into the water.

It can swim very well.

Some animals can see better at night than when the sun is out. Animals with this ability are called nocturnal animals. Two such animals of the rain forest are the **tarsier** and the **loris**.

The cute little creature in this picture is a **tarsier**. Each one of its eyes is larger than the animal's entire brain! These amazing eyes help it to see at night when it does all of its hunting for food.

Tarsiers love to jump around.

They can jump up to six feet.

But this **loris** is very, very slow.

It is always careful when it moves.

Have you ever heard of a monkey with five arms?

The **spider monkey** may not have five arms, but it uses its tail just like an extra arm. The tip of its tail can support the entire weight of its body.

A spider monkey moves through the trees using its hands, feet, and tail. This makes the monkey look like a spider crawling on a web.

Spider monkeys live in the trees.

They like to eat fruit and nuts.

They have a pink face when they are born.

   The tropical rain forests of the world are in danger due to deforestation.

Deforestation is when huge areas of the rain forest are cut down for lumber, or when the land is burned to clear it for cattle and crops. With no trees to protect it, the soil is washed away by rain or baked hard by the sun. Once this has happened the rain forest will never grow back. Without the trees the rain forest animals will have no home.

Cleared Forest Being Burned

⊙ Many people are working to save the rain forest.

We can help by letting people know we care.

It's not too late to save the trees and animals of the rain forest.

Spider Monkeys drinking from Balsa Flower

Much of the rain forest is still unexplored. New and mysterious creatures are being discovered all the time. There are so many interesting plants that scientists don't have time to investigate them all. Many of these plants may hold the cure to deadly diseases.

Segama River, Malaysia

There is still a lot more we can learn from the rain forest.

There are animals and plants there that no human has ever seen!

If you liked
***About The Rain Forest*, here is another *We Both Read*™ Book you are sure to enjoy!**

Over 20 different kinds of insects are featured in this non-fiction book in the *We Both Read*™ series. With 40 pages of amazing photographs of the insect world, this book relates fascinating facts about these six-legged creatures that will enthrall children and parents alike!